I0153557

THE
GRATITUDE LIST

Thanking those who have meant the most

DR. MARIO PAVICIC

The Gratitude List
Thanking Those Who Have Meant The Most

Copyright © 2015 by Dr. Mario Pavicic
All rights reserved.

Published in the United States of America. No part of this book may be used or reproduced in any manner whatsoever without the written permission of the publisher.

ISBN 13: 978-0-692-40557-4

Interior & Cover Design: Surf Point Direct, San Diego, CA

Printed in the United States of America

10 9 8 7 6 5 4 3 2 1
First Version

Dedication
For my family

Testimonials

"Dr. Mario has touched my life through his unexpected acts of gratitude both towards me, my family and nearly every person with whom he comes into contact."

–M.L.

"Observing Dr. Mario's acts of gratitude to nearly everyone he meets has taught me that love is in the heart."

–T.W.

"Dr. Mario reminds us all that the greatest gifts in life are tied by heartstrings and a simple act of gratitude."

–S.S.

"Whether you have just had a huge success, you're feeling down, or life has just thrown you a curve, Dr. Mario's book will show you how to harness the power of gratitude."

–A.D.

"Dr. Mario lives gratitude every day in every part of his life. His personal kindness has inspired me to be kinder and more appreciative to those who are important in my life."

–J.O.

"Want to feel great today? Want your life to feel more meaningful? Want to make a difference? Dr. Mario has the answer: share your gratefulness to others. He did it with me and made a life-long-friend."

–S.B.

"I love the simplicity of Dr. Mario's message: STOP and be thankful to all those who make your life wonderful! He did it with me and my life has been enriched."

–S.P

"Dr. Mario's book has taught me that if there is just one thing I need to do today it is to express my gratitude. It has enhanced every one of my business and life relationships."

–Dr. Ron Arndt, THE DENTAL COACH©

Acknowledgements

I dedicate this book to those whom I have dedicated my life to: my family. My father, Juraj; my mother, Katica; my brother, Boris; and my children: Julianna, Matthew and Nick. I hope my children will pass this book on to Pavicics for generations to come.

I also dedicate this book to all those who are mentioned in these pages. A sincere thank you for all you have done for me throughout my life. I would not be the man I am today without your influence.

I thank Kelly Epperson for finally inspiring me to create this book.

I am grateful for Coach Ron Arndt, Dr. Ed Bice and Dr. Tom Thomas for always pushing me to be my very best.

Introduction

Many years ago, I attended a Peter Lowe seminar that featured a speaker named Zig Ziglar. Zig strutted across the stage with great enthusiasm and, in his long Southern drawl, shouted out to the audience, "Who is on your gratitude list?"

He then proceeded to explain what people in his life he was grateful for and why they were placed on this esteemed list. Zig's words have stayed with me ever since that day.

I have indeed been truly grateful for the people who made me the man I am today. I've always remembered and appreciated those people, but did I regularly tell or show them? The answer was most assuredly no.

The small question that Zig asked had a big impact and led me to create an actual list, on paper, of the people who somehow shaped my life. Many people, in a small way or great way, have helped me get where I am today.

Creating my Gratitude List has been life changing. To recognize how much others have helped me has given me greater appreciation for my life and the people in it. I bet you can say the same.

What I have done in this book is share my own Gratitude List and give you a guide on how to create your own. It is my hope that this book will prompt you to create your own Gratitude List and cause you to think about and thank all those people in your life, who have offered help, love, support, friendship or guidance along the way.

The idea of the Gratitude List is also to serve as a reminder that no one has accomplished a great life alone.

When your list is complete, my wish is for you to look at it often and say to yourself, and to those on the paper in front of you, "Thank you for all you have done and have been to me."

Who should you include?

The task of looking back on your life and remembering all the people who have been involved in it may seem like a daunting task. You may not have thought of some people in years, and in fact some you may have downright forgotten. Don't worry. Simply reading this book will guide you back to remembering them.

Also, by reading the tributes to those individuals who have been important in my life, you may be inspired to remember even more of those who have made a difference for you or who have deeply influenced you.

I have broken down the list into categories to make it easier to trigger and organize your thoughts.

Some categories are obvious, like family, friends, teachers, and spouses. Some, like business influences and employees may not be as self-evident, and others, like in-laws and ex-spouses might get the reaction, "Are you kidding me?"

As you go through the categories the first time, simply write down the names of the people in each category that might be on your list, and then you can reflect later.

How many people should be on your list?

The answer is, "It does not matter. The sky is the limit."

It all depends on you and your life. You may only have one or two people who have greatly influenced your life; or you may have fifty-five on your list, or a hundred and fifty-five. The number of people is not the issue.

This Gratitude List is a living, moving entity. You can add people throughout your life. Do not feel badly if your list is small, and do not feel like you are too mushy by adding everyone you know. It is up to you. It is your list.

What did they do to be on the Gratitude List?

That is entirely up to you.

You can ask yourself questions like, "What or how much should the person have done to be on the list?" or "What is the meaning of "deeply influenced?"" or you can simply trust your gut. Follow your heart.

I have always looked at it that if this person had not come into my life, I would not be the person I am today. Another way to look at it is, if this person suddenly disappeared from my life, I would be wounded, feel a great loss, and my life would not be the same.

These ponderings are meant to be used in a positive manner. You can take it to any level you want. Sometimes people we are grateful for are strangers. Take an extreme example. If you were in an automobile accident and became paralyzed, you would not be the same person you are today. The person that caused the accident is a key figure in your life and had a great influence on it, but you may not consider putting them on your Gratitude List. However, if you feel that this event made you a better person and somehow changed your life for the better, then by all means put this person on your list.

We may sometimes never know the name of a person that affected us greatly, or we may not remember their name. It may be someone you met on an airplane, and you never asked their name, yet they inspired you to do great things. It could be any crazy way someone came into your life. They may not have been a long-lasting presence, but they somehow changed your life . There are no rules here and there is always room for the "John or Jane Doe" on your list.

This is your list. Be open to all the names that pop up for you.

Living or Deceased

Your list most likely will contain several deceased people. Just because a person is no longer living does not mean they should not be included. You may not be able to send them a card or give them a call, but you can thank them in your heart, your mind, and even publicly given the right opportunity.

The purpose is to feel the gratitude. We all remember our loved ones in different ways. There is no right or wrong. My mother goes to the cemetery every week to visit my dad and brother. I do not like going to cemeteries; they tend to bring me down and remind me of our mortality. Instead, I have pictures and rituals that make me remember daily those whom I have lost, family members and others. I think of my father every day as I parent my kids. I think of my brother during the day, every day, in some way. Every morning when I walk into my current office, I remember the man who sold me my first dental practice and I think how proud he would have been seeing what it has become.

Thank those who are not around anymore simply by remembering them. You can also imagine them feeling proud of who you have become and how they helped you on your path.

Gratitude List Categories

Your categories can be whatever you choose. And you don't have to categorize at all. This is just my way of helping you get started, helping you think of all the people who have made an impact on your life.

God

We all hear athletes after a big win thank God, or Jesus, for helping them. (I always wonder why He helped them beat a Cleveland team.)

Maybe your Gratitude List will include thanks to a higher being or Higher Power or God or Spirit. Spirituality is, in my opinion, a great start to finding gratitude in your heart. If this is important to you, then without a doubt place the greater being on your list.

Since each person's relationship with God is different, I will not talk specifics in this book, but God is on my list and I thank Him every day for the life I have. You can express your gratitude in whatever way resonates with you.

Family

Depending on your own life, this category might be the largest percentage of your list. For many people, it is easiest to start with family members because that is where we got our start in life. Thanking one's parents seems like a given, but it is understood that nothing is a "should" and some things may not always be easy or obvious. Not everyone feels close to their parents.

Even if you do not/did not have a close relationship with your mother and/or father, there may be some way you can think of a glimmer of gratitude. Maybe the hardships formed you into the strong person you are today. Maybe they were harsh but you appreciate your strong work ethic that resulted. You may discover that you have something there to write a gratitude.

However, DO NOT feel like you have to thank anyone, or include anyone on your list, no matter what their tie or relationship was to you.

The Gratitude List is genuine and heartfelt, a tool to feel good. It is not a forced exercise in any way, shape, or form. Again, this is an exercise to bring up good feelings, not hard feelings. Focus on those who have shaped you and helped you. Express your gratitude to them. It will have a very powerful effect on you.

Since the category of Family can be quite large, break it down. Parents. Siblings. Grandparents. Aunts/Uncles. Cousins.

Parents can include your birth parents, adoptive parents, step-parents, foster parents. Siblings can include brothers and sisters, half-brothers, step-sisters, etc. You get the idea. Sometimes family is blood, sometimes family is blended.

I know grandparents will be on the top of the Gratitude List for many people. I know they will be for my kids. I never knew any of my grandparents. They died before I was born.

It is my wish for you that those of you who have siblings, to cherish them. Even though they might be different and miles separate you, keep them in your hearts and minds. You may not be best friends, but you can probably find some gratitude there no matter how strained a relationship may be. Some people find a Gratitude List can help heal wounds.

Children

The first category of family above included a lot of extended family, those we were born into or adopted into or our mom or dad married into. There are many ways you end up with a lot of family members and not all of them will go on your Gratitude List. Instead of lumping our own children into the Family category, I pulled Children out separately.

If you do have children, you know what an impact it can be to be a parent to our children. For me, my kids have been my greatest lessons in life and love. My children hold a very special place on my Gratitude List. Maybe you do not have kids, or maybe your children have not been that kind of relationship for you. There is no judging here. These categories are here to help you craft your list.

If you do include children on your list, you can choose to write your gratitude to your children individually or collectively. There is no right or wrong. There is only expression.

Spouse or Partner

Many people will find that their spouse or partner is the first person they want to thank in their Gratitude List. The person that you choose to spend your life with usually does have a significant influence on your life. If you are filled with gratitude for your sweetheart, take your time writing your thanks. It will make you feel wonderful.

Without a doubt, this category will be the most important decision of your life. If all goes well, you will spend more time with this person than any other. I look around at marriages today and unfortunately, too many times it turns from this category to the one below.

For those who do have a special person in your life, suffice to say that he or she will be with you through thick and thin, good and bad, children, and into old age and retirement. Your spouse/partner doesn't need to be thanked and shown gratitude just on occasions and on special days; they need to be shown gratitude every day. They do not need to be written down on a piece of paper, but instead indelibly tattooed onto your heart, mind and soul.

Ex-Spouses

This category, like all the categories, are up to your discretion. Just because a marriage does not last forever does not mean it was a failure. You may choose to thank your ex-spouse for your children, for being a support to you when you needed, or helping you grow.

It can be very freeing to feel gratitude for an ex-spouse. Yes, there are painful memories too, but feeling some gratitude for him or her can make you feel lighter.

Friends

We meet friends in all kinds of various ways throughout our life. Some kinds of friends will be broken down in other categories, and sometimes we also consider a sibling a best friend. It does not matter how you categorize. Use this as a trigger to get your creative and grateful juices flowing.

Friends could be childhood friends, classmates, coworkers, colleagues, running buddies, coffee shop pals, and on and on. There is no end to how friends can come into your life. You might meet someone at the checkout line at the grocery story and become great friends.

Take some time to think of the friends who have made a difference in your life. You can define "friend" in many ways. It doesn't have to be someone you see or talk to every day or even every week, month or year. Make a list of all the friends that you feel have made a great impact in your life. Think back from when you were a child to now. Look at old photo albums, yearbooks and letters.

Include as many as you choose in your Gratitude List.

Neighbors

You may or may not have been influenced by your neighbors. It depends on where you lived and what kind of relationships developed. You may have been profoundly affected by a kind neighbor when you were growing up or you may have relied tremendously on your neighbors in your adult life.

Everyone's life is different. The categories provided for you are to stimulate your thinking, not make you feel pressured to add people.

In-laws

Many people are very close to their in-laws, and can remain close even after death or divorce of their spouse. Of course, some people are not close to their in-laws (and hence, the classic mother-in-law jokes). As always, include those people on your list for whom you feel gratitude.

I had two brother-in-laws and a mother- and father-in-law that were in my life but are really not anymore due to my divorce. We are still on good terms and see each other at the kids' events. I am grateful that they always treated me with respect and kindness during the time I was married. I will always be kind in return.

My sister-in-law, the wonderful woman who married my brother is definitely on my list. In-laws can become family.

Listen to your heart as to who to include, and that applies to all the categories.

Teachers

No matter where you are or what you are doing, a teacher has probably made a positive influence on you. Some people have many teachers that impacted. Some have just one. Think back to the teachers you have had over the years. Does anyone make your Gratitude List?

Coaches

Without a doubt, many people will have a sports coach on your list. Sports coaches can be some of the greatest influences in our lives.

Professional Relationships

Just about everyone can attribute some of their success at work to help they received from someone in their field. Co-workers, bosses, mentors, staff can all be on this list. "Famous" mentors who have influenced you can be included as well.

Institutions, Companies, & Organizations

We can also be grateful for an institution or organization that has greatly affected us. This can include colleges and universities, employers, and nonprofit organizations where you might volunteer, or any other entity. It is not just specific individuals we are grateful for, the organizations and institutions of our life shape us too. Include any on your list where you feel deeply indebted for the opportunities and life-growth it has given you.

Now allow me to share my Gratitude List. My intent is to offer up some "real-life" examples to help you create your own list. Some people have long stories, some do not. You may choose to write a story about those on your list as a gratitude exercise or simply having them down on your list is enough The following sections are a tribute to my Gratitude List. I hope reading the stories will make you laugh, cry, reminisce or simply make you feel good inside. Enjoy my Gratitude List. More importantly, enjoy creating your Gratitude List. The process of writing down your gratitudes can change you and your life!

MY GRATITUDE LIST

My Mother

Katica Pavicic

The second person that athletes thank after God when winning the big game is usually "Mom." After the obvious points of giving us life and dealing with heartburn for nine months, moms do a lot. Many will argue that their mom is the best mom in the world, and they can prove it. I would like to throw my mom into the mix for your consideration.

My mother, Katica, was born on a farm in Croatia and did all the duties that typical ethnic moms from that era did. She would farm, milk cows, feed pigs, take care of kids, and walk the laundry down to the river on a basket on her head, just to name a few chores.

After we came to America, she took a job in downtown Cleveland cleaning offices at night. She would leave about 5pm, take the bus to work, and then arrive home sometime after midnight, well after I had fallen asleep. Being an avid stamp collector, I would wake up and run to the table to find stamps she had ripped off of envelopes for me. Needless to say, with her job in an international business building, I had the most envious stamp collection in my school.

My mother taught me how to thank God, and taught me to pray in Croatian at night as I fell asleep. She is the most kind and gentle person I know. While my dad taught with the heavy hand, she taught me with love and tenderness. My mother lost her firstborn son to leukemia over fifteen years ago. I thought it would kill her, but it didn't because she had more work to do with her two new grandchildren. After my father had a stroke, she took care of him at home, by herself, for several years. When he died, she forged on. She then had to watch her second son (me) go through a painful divorce.

After my dad passed away, Mom moved in with me and my three kids, and became a mother to them . Today, she is still our rock. At 77 years old, she still picks up my son Nick from school. Years ago, it was all three of the kids. She wakes up at 6:30 a.m., and still insists on making their lunches. She shops, cooks and mends wounds just like she did for me 40-plus years ago.

I am not certain about many things, but I am certain about one. There is not a person out there who has met my mom that doesn't love or respect her. She travels with us, and still finds the strength to lumber through the streets of Ireland, the tight trails of Mammoth Cave, and the crazy crowds of Disney.

Every time I feel like my life is tough, I sit and think of all she has been through and how she stills smiles and remains positive. I don't know what the kids and I would do without her. I lay down each night and thank God for my mom and, on some nights when it is quiet, I will hear her praying in Croatian with one of my kids before they fall asleep. Thanks, Mom. You are the best person I know!

My Father

Juraj Pavicic

My father, like my mother, was born on a farm in Croatia (next village over). However, he had bigger dreams and aspirations than living out his life on a poor farm in a communist country. When his first child was born, his dreams got even bigger, and when his second son was born, the spark really ignited. I could write an entire book about my dad, and maybe someday I will, but for now I will just write a small summary. I guess I never realized how influential he was in my life. Each day I realize it more.

Many of the things my father said to me when I was young made no sense to me then, but now resonate loud and clear. Much of what he said took me over 40 years to figure out, and most everything he said, in one way or the other, has come true.

One of the greatest things I remember about him, other than all of our fishing and hunting trips, is the time we spent together fixing everything ever invented. The man could fix everything from a simple transistor radio to a commercial rooftop air conditioning unit, and anything on a car.

If there was speed dial back then, he would have been on many people's list. When a call came, I would grab the green metal tool box and off we would go. It would be one of our Croatian friends' refrigerator or furnace, or maybe someone's car wasn't running or their TV was on the fritz.

No matter what the circumstance, my dad had a solution. He never took money from a single person for his services; I think his payment was a sampling of some food, a glass of homemade wine and to listen to one of his stories. Learning from my dad was priceless. By the way, my brother got all the repair smarts. I am much handier with a dental handpiece than any screwdriver.

One of the best things I remember, that seemed not so great at the time, is that my dad was always around. Back then I wished many times he wasn't there so I could do what I wanted. He never really went out with friends or took trips by himself, other than a few trips to Croatia over the years. His words still resonate with me today: "Where I go, my kids go."

I hear many people say that their dad was never around. I was fortunate my dad was always there when I needed him. Fishing on our boat on Lake Erie on early Sunday mornings as a kid is a great memory. He missed only one or two games of my basketball career. Eighth grade to senior year, home or away, his face was always in the crowd.

It always meant a lot to know that he was in the stands. He was always there to support me in all things. I think his proudest moment was when I was accepted to Case Western Reserve University Dental School. I think all that he ever dreamed of becoming, I had done for him.

My dad was also a very tough man; he demanded obedience and hard work. He also demanded excellence, and one of the greatest driving forces in my life was not letting him down. Unfortunately, like many ethnic dads, his delivery was some-

THE GRATITUDE LIST | 21

times not the best, and I have tried to avoid that in my own parenting. I tell my kids that you learn many ways to do things correctly from your parents, and sometimes you also learn how not to do things.

He was the greatest American patriot I have ever known. He chastised our fellow immigrants if they ever bad-mouthed America. He cheered for our American teams and cried at Ronald Reagan's stirring speeches when America helped end the communism he had escaped.

I am grateful that my dad lived to meet all three of his grandchildren. I often wish he was in the stands watching his grandchildren play basketball or teaching them the correct way to bait a fishing hook. He died before his time. He will undoubtedly be the greatest influence in my life. He truly made me who I am today. Thanks, Dad! I miss you!

My one and only brother

Boris Pavicic

Being a 12-year-old immigrant kid in the 70's was not easy. My brother, Boris, who was 11 years older than me, said one of his greatest adventures was riding his bike to the neighboring village, with only moonlight as a beacon, to tell the midwife that my mother had gone into labor with me. This type of devotion was what he would show me my entire life. He was oftentimes just as much a father to me as a brother. Boris took the brunt of my dad's anger over the years as I sat back and took mental notes of what angered dad. I became an expert at avoiding those moments with our father.

Boris and I were never at the same points in our lives. When he was in college, I was in 2nd grade. When I was in dental school, he was starting his own business. I remember all the little things he did that you don't think are a big deal at the time, but years later, matter a lot, like listening to "The Shadow" in bed late at night, eating ice cream until we were sick, and sticking up for me when I needed him to.

My brother and I had only one spat in our lives. It was over a seemingly dumb Croatian card game where we played on teams. I was paired up with my cousin opposing my brother. I ranted, whooped it up and jeered at Boris as I high-fived my partner for kicking my brother's butt at cards. As we left the house, Boris grabbed my arm in a fit of rage and told me I was his brother, the only brother I would ever have, and I should never make fun of his misfortune and should always support him. "We are a team, not anyone else." I of course bawled my eyes out, and I never forgot that night. From that day on he was my best "teammate."

When we were finally both established in our careers, we started going on vacations together. We went on a weeklong adventure to Washington, DC, and then a 2,500 mile trip from Vegas to Utah to Arizona. We never made it to vacation number three. My brother contracted Acute Lymphocytic Leukemia at the age of 41. He only made it nine months and then, in the blink of an eye, my brother and best friend was gone.

Boris died exactly one month after my first son, Matt, was born and Matt bears my brother's name as his middle name. The last thing I said to Boris before he died was, "Thank you for being my big brother and taking care of me, and don't worry, I will live for the both of us." I think of my brother every day and try to live up to that promise.

Thank you, Boris. I love you and miss you every day.

My kids

I always looked forward to becoming a father and being a dad has been, and is, one of my greatest joys. We brought Julianna home in 1997, Matthew followed 14 months later, and Nick arrived four years after that.

My kids are simply the greatest reason for everything I do in my life. Every step I take, every breath I take, I am thinking of how I can make their life and success greater than mine. I thank God every day that they are healthy, fun-loving, well-adjusted kids that keep me moving.

I would not trade driving them to school every day, coaching my boys in basketball, cheering and agonizing watching my daughter play basketball, banging my head on the table at the next school project I had to help with. I will never regret choosing to take them to the movies or just staying home instead of going on a date or out with friends. I want my kids to remember that I was there for them whenever they needed, as my father was for me.

We have traveled the United States and the world together on great adventures. I have taken them to black-tie affairs when they were younger than seven years old and was never embarrassed or ashamed to do so. Where I go, my kids go. As I write this, Julianna, is a senior in high school and Matt will follow next year. The old adage "enjoy them, they grow up fast" is so true. I see a different part of me in each of them, I only hope they are the best parts.

I have been a single parent for over ten years now and I may have not been perfect in my parenting, but I have given them the basics, like a loving household, laughter, adventure and stability. I cry every time I think of all we have been through together, good and bad. I look forward to seeing them become happy adults who will let their old man babysit their kids someday.

Thank you, Julianna, Matt and Nick. Our story is just beginning. I love you all more than life itself.

My aunts and uncles

I was lucky to have five aunts and uncles. I didn't know three of them very well because they lived in Croatia, but from them I have some of my favorite cousins, who live in Croatia, Germany, and Canada. I am closest to my mother's two brothers, Uncle Slavko (deceased) and Uncle Joe. Uncle Joe was the reason we came to America.

Uncle Joe had come to America to escape communism and, with the help of the Catholic Church, moved to Cleveland. He sponsored us to come to America and we lived with him for the first few months when we arrived in the US.

Uncle Joe is a quiet but fun man. He has one of the sweetest hearts of any man I know. One of the most hilarious moments I remember was when he introduced me to hot peppers at Huntington Beach. The experience was similar to being burned on the oven as a kid – it's one of those things you always remember, no matter how old you were when it happened. I have loved hot, spicy peppers and food ever since.

He married my Aunt Kathy, and the two of them have been a great help and influence in my life. They are a part of my children's lives and activities. Whenever my mother and I need help of any kind they are always there for us. My aunt's puff pastry dessert is my all time favorite!

Thank you to my Uncle Joe and Aunt Kathy for all your help and support.

My cousins

I have eight first cousins and many second and third cousins all over the world. Three cousins are part of my Gratitude List. Ivan came to America when I was six years old. He lived in our duplex house in Cleveland with us.

As immigrants many times do, our family liked being close. When we moved to Brooklyn, Ohio, soon after my Uncle Joe and Aunt Kathy did too, followed by Cousin Ivan. We were all a five minute walk from each other. Ivan was fifteen years older than me, was my ride and my surrogate brother, since my brother was gone from the house by then.

Ivan and his sister, my cousin Mira, were the largest reason for my soccer and ping pong prowess, as we spent many days of my childhood in their backyard. We used to go to the beach and movies, and they made me laugh a lot. Today Ivan's son, Johnny, is my son's Matt's Confirmation sponsor, and my daughter was in his daughter, Kristina's wedding recently. Thanks, Ivan and Mira, for making my childhood and teenage years what they were.

My Aunt Kathy's son (also named Mario) came to America in the fourth grade. He is four months younger than me, so I joke that he was named after me. I finally had a cousin/playmate that was my age. We had a lot of fun in the summers.

Mario was and still is a quiet and sometimes solitary person, and I, on the other hand, was a loud and, at times, annoying little kid. This caused its share of friction. I really abused cousin Mario way more than I should have. On more than one occasion, he yelled, "I'm not your cousin anymore!" but we always made up.

He was the one kid I could always count on to hang out with me and make my life fun. We still see each other on the holidays and reminisce about the old days. Thanks, Cousin Mario, and sorry....

My ex-spouse

Ugh, this is a tough one. However, how can I leave out the person who gave me the four greatest moments of my life? Even though divorce is painful and heartbreaking, I choose to focus on the four greatest memories: my wedding day and the birth of my three children.

I remember being so happy on Sept 23rd, 1995, ready to start my life with the woman I loved so much. Throughout death and illness we supported each other. We worked together for close to ten years and never argued at work or about work. It was really quite amazing all the things we did together. We always got along during our marriage, no fights to speak of, and no pan-throwing arguments.

Just because something does not last forever does not mean that it was not real or wonderful. I am thankful for what we had. We still get along and it's been more than two decades since we met. Thanks, Angie, for giving birth to our three wonderful children and giving me some of the best days of my life.

Teachers

Don Lewis

Mr. Lewis or "Screwy Louie," as we sometimes called him, was one of my favorite teachers. He made my list for the simple fact that I had him as a teacher in many classes and he made me believe I was the best, most complete student in the history of Brooklyn High School. He saw greatness in me and always affirmed that I would do something big with my life someday. He treated me differently, in the fact that he talked to me like an adult from tenth grade on. He really did make me believe in myself. Thanks, Mr. Lewis.

Richard Zeitlow

I never quite understood at the time why my high school biology teacher helped me so much in getting where I am today. He saw my potential. My entire senior year was filled with awards, banquets, checks, and plaques because of him. I remember Mr. Zeitlow would walk up to me in the hallway and say, "Mario, I entered your essay in a contest for a scholarship. Hope you don't mind." Inevitably, I would get a call that I won first place, some money, or a plaque, and I would receive a letter to please come to a dinner to get it. So away Mr. Zeitlow, my parents and I would go to dinner.

Off the top of my head, I remember he helped me win five awards and over $2,000 in college money. The greatest moment we had was when I was applying at Case Western Reserve University for a four-year scholarship worth $4,000 a year (a big amount in 1986). We had to bring the teacher who wrote the recommendation with us to the interview. One of the proudest moments of my life was when he was asked, "How often do you see a student like Mario in your high school?" "Once in a lifetime," was his reply. The scholarship was mine.

He became my patient as soon as I bought my first practice, and we remained close for many years. We were always joking, "When is our next dinner?" Thanks, Mr. Zietlow, for believing in me.

Lou Syroney

I doubt that many people will have their high school principal on a Gratitude List. They were known more for yelling, paddling and disciplining students. My high school principal, Mr. Syroney, did all that (never to me…), but he also gave me the belief that I could accomplish great things. He treated me like an adult, saying, "Let's go have a talk in my office. How are you doing? Are you on target for your goals? If you need anything, let me know."

Mr. Syroney is still a patient of mine today.. His other career was as a basketball referee, and he even came to my daughter's district game last year. I always like catching up with Lou on the latest gossip from good old Brooklyn High School. Thank you, Mr. Syroney.

Dr. Marius Laniauskas

Once you get to professional school, the stakes get bigger; not only the cost, but the importance. I arrived at Case Western

Reserve University (CWRU)Dental School a 20-year-old boy, and left a 24-year-old confident man and dentist, mostly because of one man, Dr. Marius Laniauskas.

My first encounter with him was not good. I didn't like what he had told me about a project, "You can do a lot better than that!" How dare he tell me that?! I had been a star student and was used to accolades. Needless to say, I avoided him the rest of sophomore year.

When I found out that I was to be his student in the clinic for the next two years, I cringed. The next two years, I learned more from him about dentistry and life than I could ever have imagined. Dr. Laniauskas taught me compassion, hand skills, how to treat patients with confidence, how to be a family man someday, and also how to teach. Simply, he gave me the technical and life tools that have brought me to where I am today.

He is still one of my best friends and we get together often. I still learn from him. We have been traveling all around the country watching March Madness basketball for the past fourteen years. I always look forward to March and a trip with one of my best friends. Thanks, Marius, for making me the man I am.

Coaches

I have only one coach that makes my list. I currently coach basketball for my two sons, and I have always taken it seriously. A coach is in a powerful position to make or break an athlete. One single person made me love basketball more than any other and, to this day, 30-plus years later, I still use his words and hear him yelling, "Boards!"

Mr. Ron Szudy is a god in Brooklyn High School lore for his incredible history teaching and football coaching. But for one year, when no one else would, he took on the position of ninth grade basketball coach. To this day, I really don't know if he had any great basketball knowledge; I can't remember any intricate plays or defenses. I do remember that his pre-game, halftime, and post-game speeches brought the best out of our team and led to a magical year.

I remember the look of pride he had on his face when I put in the game-winning basket at the buzzer against Buckeye High School, beating them for the first time in school history at any basketball level (still my life's greatest sports moment).

Coach Szudy taught us how to play together, hustle, and never give up. We flat out wanted to win for him! He taught us how to lose with pride and how to always show sportsmanship.

To this day, I will never forget when we lost one of our final games together against an undefeated Lutheran West team who had beaten us by 30 points earlier in the season. We led by six points with one minute left and lost it at the end. I must have had 15 rebounds that game. To a man, we all cried in the locker room. Mr. Szudy just hugged each of us and told us that he was proud of us and, win or lose, we were the greatest sports team he had ever coached.

At the sports banquet, as he spoke about that game, he told the audience, "In that game, Mario turned from a boy into a man." I'm not sure, but I think those simple words catapulted me into the high school success I had in school and sports. Thank you, Mr. Szudy. I will never forget the lessons you taught.

Professional Relationships

Soon after my dental school was completed, I went into a residency at Metro Health Medical Center. That is where my list begins.

Dr. Leonard P. Weiss

Dr. Lenny Weiss hired me as a resident in 1993. He quickly showed great confidence in me and allowed me to work on difficult cases and be the leader of my group. Trusting someone to do a job and then letting them do it really makes a person grow in their field. I quickly became the highest producer in the group.

At the end of my residency, he wanted me to stay on and be the Chief Resident. That offer meant a lot to me. Sadly, I had to decline. Lenny and I are still good friends, and I love seeing him at dental events with his wonderful wife, Sandy. I love them both. Thanks, Lenny!

Dr. Marko Kuhar

I remember my dad bragging about Dr.Kuhar, how nice he was, what a nice life he had, what a great career dentistry was. Maybe those subliminal messages led me to choose dentistry as a career.

All the Croatians and Serbians went to Dr. Kuhar; he didn't speak fluent Croatian but knew enough to get by with his patients. When he knew that I was going to dental school, he started joking about us working together someday. Those conversations got serious my senior year and we started planning for the future.

We planned that I would slowly take over his office and eventually buy it from him. He started telling patients that I was coming a year in advance of my arrival! Six months into my residency, we found out he had cancer and our working together would never happen.

I went with Dr. Kuhar to some of his cancer treatments and we laughed a lot and cried sometimes. We started discussing the full purchase of his practice and building. On July 1, I started my private practice career at his practice of 30-plus years. He called and wished me luck, and said he knew I would become a success. He died two days later.

I never got to work with Dr. Kuhar, but from his hard work I built what I have today, one of the most successful dental practices in the country. Many of the patients he took care of for more than thirty years, I have now been taking care of for over twenty. I still take care of his incredible wife, Mary Lou, his children, their spouses and his grandchildren. I am indebted to the Kuhar family for giving me the start of my wonderful career. Thank you, Dr. Kuhar, and the Kuhar family.

Sarah Gentile

Along with the practice, I inherited a well-seasoned staff. Without them, I would probably not have done as well as I did. Dr. Kuhar believed in me and, soon, so did they.

My assistant Sarah was an incredible woman with the hardest work ethic I have ever seen. Whatever had to be done, she did. She knew every single patient and who they were related to, their favorite appointment time and favorite food (kidding about the food). She was always in a friendly and great mood. She became like a second mother to me and helped me get where I am today. Sadly, Sarah died suddenly, just a short time before we opened our new office. Thank you, Sarah, for all your support, I could not have done it without you!

Dr. Casey O'Conor & Dr. Tom Murphy

In the world of dentistry, as in many other professions, there are specialists who rely on general dentists to send them patients. It is sometimes difficult to find a perfect fit for a specialist who not only takes care of the patients you send, but also takes care of you when needed.

I was lucky enough to find two great clinicians and friends, and they helped me get where I am. The first is the orthodontist who was close to my first office, Dr. Casey O'Conor. Casey has not only taken care of my patients, but also my kids. We play a few rounds of golf every year and he is always the first one to sign up and donate to my foundation, The Boris Pavicic Leukemia Foundation. Casey has an incredible Irish family. I will miss seeing Casey every 6 weeks after my youngest is done with his braces. I guess we will have to play more golf! Thanks, Casey, for all the support and fun over the past 20 years.

Dr. Murphy, along with Dr. O'Conor, immediately welcomed me to the area with lunches and better yet, sports tickets. Like Dr. O'Conor, Dr. Murphy was not the type of guy who just wanted the business; he became a real friend. He invited me to play basketball in his group soon after I started in my practice. Now, this may not seem like a big deal for many of you, but for a basketball player to be invited into a close knit group of guys who had been playing for years, it meant a lot. Along with it came invites to his home for parties and many rounds of golf. Whenever and however I need him he is there for me, professionally or personally. My favorite saying of his is "Whatever you need, Mario."

Thank you, Tom, for all the support and great times we have shared and I hope there are many more to come.

Dr. Bob Hirsch

Dr. Bob was the man who interviewed me for my first teaching job in the clinics at CWRU School of Dental Medicine. What a great man he is. He taught me a lot about life and helped me through my most difficult times. Later, as he left the school, he lobbied and helped me get appointed to the Head of Practice Management program at the school, a position I still have today. Bob is now the Dean of a dental school, a position he well deserves. I will never forget the special hot sausages he used to make for me that nearly killed me one night! Bob always has some great story to tell, about rat slapping in Erie as a kid or some great sausage or beer he tried or made. I miss hanging out with him. However he is in a better place……. Florida! Thank you Bob for giving me the chance.

Dr. Jerold Goldberg

Dr. Jerry Goldberg, Dean of CWRU School of Dental Medicine, allowed me to pursue my passion for teaching young dental students how to become successful clinicians and businesspeople. Instead of allowing non-dental MBA instructors teach dental students about the business of dentistry, he allowed me to do it. Today it is one of the highest-rated classes (by the dental students) in the school curriculum.

Jerry led my alma mater from obscurity to fame. My first encounter with the future Dean was my senior year in dental school. As President of Student Council, I asked him to please move his exam back a couple of days in order to make our lives easier. He looked me straight in the face and said, "No."

I don't believe I talked to him again until he was Dean four years later. From then on, I talked to him a lot. As a matter of fact, I just introduced him as the Distinguished Alumnus of the Year at Case Western Reserve University. Dr. Goldberg shows real passion for the school he graduated from, and has stayed there his entire career. I don't think anyone could have done the job in the way he has done it. I think he will go down as the greatest Dean of our dental school, and I am proud to have helped him in some small way to attain that distinction.

Thanks, Dr. Goldberg, for having me teach these kids how to be successful in practice and in life.

Dr. Mark Morin

Many people attribute their professional success to a mentor or a coach. My inspiration and model for how I wanted to live and practice came from an unexpected place: Detroit, Michigan. More specifically, Southfield, Michigan. My business partner, Tom, and I had an interest in doing CEREC dental restorations, so we attended a seminar given by Dr. Mark Morin. By the end of the lecture, we were sold!

Dr. Mark's enthusiasm and knowledge hooked us. We came to learn a lot from him and we also have had a lot of great times. From Michigan to Ohio, Las Vegas to New Orleans, Atlantis, Grand Cayman and St. Maarten, we followed and learned about dentistry and about how to enjoy life. We mirrored his office in many ways and I still believe his teachings were the single greatest reason we are where we are today.

Thanks, Mark, for making my practice and in many ways, my life, what it is today and teaching me how not to be a "loser." (Inside joke!)

My Staff

No great business of any kind, from Google to Apple to the mom and pop store, has attained greatness without dedicated employees. I have had many staff members in my 20+ years of dentistry, and I remember each one and what they meant to me. They each taught me lessons on business, psychology or human needs.

Currently, Tom and I have nine employees and our business could never be as successful as it is without their hard work and dedication. Some employers forget to thank their employees, as I do on occasion. It would behoove us to make them feel appreciated each day. They are truly what makes our business tick. Thank you, all, especially my current staff for all you have done for me and my family. We truly couldn't do it without you!

Anthony Robbins

I remember the day I confided to my friend Louise how low I was feeling because my marriage was ending, what a failure I felt like, how all my dreams of family, love and the fairy tale were ending. Even though I had a great group of friends that listened, consoled and even gave advice, I felt no better. My kids were the only thing that really kept me going. I was treading water not knowing where to turn, or what could snap me out of it. Louise said, "You need to go to a Tony Robbins seminar."

I knew of Tony's work and tried to read his book years prior, but I think things like that don't sink until you need them. I searched online and signed up for his four-day seminar, "Unleash the Power Within." I went to LA with expectations of a big sales pitch sprinkled with some good information to lure me in. What I got was something that turned the tide of my life and carried me to where I am today. I walked on hot coals, climbed telephone poles, poured out my heart to strangers, danced, cried, screamed and, briefly, slept. I can't describe it in words. I drank the Kool-Aid, smoked the pipe, sat in the tent, and whatever else the nonbelievers would call it. All I know is that I bawled my eyes out on the plane ride back from LA and, when I came home, I hugged my mom and each of my kids and said, "Daddy is back!"

I was back not just physically, but mentally. I took back control of my life. I have attended many more seminars with Tony and even helped crew. Each one was more incredible then the last. With every keystroke I type, I think of all the lessons he taught me and all the friends his seminars have brought to my life. Thank you, Tony, for saving my life.

Friends

They say if you have only one or two true friends in life you are a lucky person. I have had the privilege of having many. Some came and spent only a short time in my life but had a great influence.

Friends, colleagues, staff, past relationships, I have lumped many people in my Friends category. I listed them all and, instead of trying to put them in impact order, I put them in alphabetical order for this book. However, I kept a few out of order for special recognition at the end. So don't worry, you are in there!

Al

Al was my brother's brother in-law. He was the first employee my brother had in his company, Medscan Services. Together, they spent many a hour traveling for work. They also hunted and golfed together. Al always had a lot of respect for

Boris and became one of his best friends. To this day, Al goes to my brother's grave and places golf balls and other little gifts on his headstone. He is the first one in line for our memorial golf outing in August for my brother, and always brings great cheer and memories. Thank you, Al, for always having a place in your heart for Boris.

Alessandra

I am lucky to have found friends from all over the world in my travels. As just stated, I attribute much of my success to the teachings of Anthony Robbins and I also attribute finding some of the greatest friends and people I know to attending Tony Robbins seminars. At the"Date with Destiny" seminar, I spent eight days finding out who I really was. In the process, I worked in a trio of people. One of my partners was Alessandra, from San Paolo, Brazil. Together we crafted our lives, desires and destinies. I will never be able to thank her enough for pushing and supporting me through this process. We still text and email regularly. Obrigado, Alessandra.

Angie

The first long-term relationship of my life started my third year of dental school. I was the second youngest student in my class, and still only 23 years old. In walked the most beautiful, big-haired blond girl I had ever seen. We spent two years to-gether and had a lot of fun in an atmosphere of high stress and great demands. I never gave her what she deserved or wanted and, in the end, due to my lack of experience in these matters, I guess as they say, I blew it. That was a long time ago and Angie is happy in in her life with her great husband and beautiful children. Thank you, Angie, for teaching me a lot about love and patience. I am glad you found happiness and success.

Dan

Dan is one of several lifelong dental school friends to whom I have remained close. He is a fraternity brother and someone who inspires me with his love of life and adventure. My family spent three spring breaks with Dan and his family in Florida at their beautiful home. Dan was also generous enough to set up one of my bucket list items when he got Super Bowl tickets for Tom and me. It turned out to be one of, if not THE, greatest Super Bowls in history. Dan always opened his home to us and it will always be one of my family's best memories. Dan is the type of friend that I don't see often, but the times I do are spent laughing and reminiscing. In the end, I leave with a great sense of joy. Thanks, Dan, for all the years of friendship.

Dr. Dave Hertel

One of my greatest passions is my dental fraternity, Delta Sigma Delta. Dave started me on the path to leadership in my local chapter and nationally. He had the belief in me to carry the torch that he lit so brightly. Dave and I golf during his trips back to Cleveland from Florida, and I see him at our national conventions. He and his wife Nancy have been some of my great fans over the years. Thanks, Dave, for believing in me to carry the Delt torch.

Dawn

Talk about love/hate relationships – Dawn was a classmate of mine in dental school and, just like all attractive females, she was the object of my affections for several years. That is, unless she was driving me nuts! Dawn and I studied together, had dinners together and sat close to each other in lab and class, but she always had a boyfriend. What I found, instead of a girlfriend, was a great friend who also helped me through the rough dental school days. We had a lot of fun with the group of friends that we had. Dawn became an Endodontist (a root canal specialist) in my area, and I send her patients from time to time. In return, she sends me sharp Number 2 pencils (inside joke). Thanks, Dawn, for helping me through dental school and giving me lasting memories.

Dawn

Many students have come and gone in my years of teaching dental school, but none quite like Dawn. Her incredible enthusiasm and love for life is truly infectious. I always look forward to talking to her because I know I am going to laugh and get in a great mood. She also has the distinction of having the most elaborate, beautiful wedding I have ever attended. She is truly a genuinely great person, and I am glad to have helped her get where she is today. Thanks, Dawn, and nothing has changed!

Diana

When I first started undergrad at CWRU in Cleveland, I was a shy, inexperienced guy when it came to girls. I wasn't allowed to really date in high school. All my so-called girlfriends

THE GRATITUDE LIST | 43

were mostly just good friends that didn't lead to much. When I started CWRU as a freshman, knowing I would leave for dental school after two years, I was there to do my business and move on. We had a freshman retreat prior to the start of classes at a camp that I can only compare to Meatballs or Camp Crystal Lake from Friday the 13th. There, my eyes locked on a tall, beautiful, teal-eyed Norwegian girl. I don't know if it was her beauty or personality that crushed me, but I spent the next week crafting a way to kiss her. I really didn't think anything would work since she was one of the most desirable women in our school and, with an 8:1 men to women ratio, I had no chance. However, we did date for a while and although it was for a short time, it created a lifetime of good memories for me. For the first time in my life, I had confidence in myself with girls. I am glad to say we are still friends to this day. She has a tremendous husband and three beautiful children. I am always glad to hear about her family's successes and hope that we always remain close friends. Thanks, Diana. Don't forget the laundry!

Everett

Everett was another one of those guys I look back and describe as "an old college buddy of mine." He was in engineering school and I was pre-dental so, after freshman chemistry, we never really had class together. However, we remained friends. I would always seem to wake him up at odd times, like 2:00 p.m. Some people just liked to sleep during the day and study all night. Everett was the type of guy that when we did something together, we always found a way to have a great time. He moved to Louisville, married a great lady, and they have two wonderful kids. We spent two Independence Day weekends with them Everett and I speak in movie code (a guy thing). Pink Panther, The Good, The Bad and The Ugly, Patton, and The Breakfast Club were all our favorites. Taking a page out of Wayne's World, our car would rock to Bohemian Rhapsody. Nix nil nah! Thanks, Everett, for all the years of friendship.

Hermina

Growing up, I guess every boy has his first big crush. Unfortunately, my first was a Canadian girl. Our families were good friends, and our dads used to fish and hunt in the old country, and then in the cottage country of Ontario. We would stop and sleep over at their house before we all tracked up North to Honey Harbour. I used to get excited when I saw the apartments that were near their house from the highway; it meant we were close. She was and still is beautiful, athletic and outgoing. She is happily married and we see each other at weddings and on Facebook. She has a great husband and three awesome kids. Thanks, Herm, for showing me that Canadian girls are great!

Jaime

Jaime and her family were all patients and one day her father asked if Jaime could observe my office since she was interested in a career in dentistry. Tom and I enjoy having students come through our office to observe and ask questions. Jaime became one of my assistants and I enjoyed being able to train her for her first real job. Jaime and her family have since moved to South Carolina but we still keep in touch. Jaime has many talents, like painting and decorating which she has done to most of my house.. Thanks Jaime for making my house more valuable and more importantly being a valuable piece of my heart.

Joe and Terri

My neighbors, Joe and Terri, have three kids; Brandi, Jeremy and Jessie. Our kids became best friends when they moved in. When I needed them the most, during my divorce years, Joe and Terri were there for me. Joe and I would take the kids to movies, camping, Kalahari. When I needed to go somewhere and leave the kids, they were there in a heartbeat, saying, "Send them right over."

Joe and Terri were one of the main reasons I stayed in this house and continue to live in the only house my kids have ever known. Julianna and Brandi became the best of friends and still are today. We still go camping every Labor Day weekend and whenever we need each other, we come running across the street. Thanks, Joe and Terri, for all you have done for my family.

John and Dawn

There are couples who come with your spouse when you get married. John and Dawn were one of those couples (Scott and Kim, below, were the other). I didn't have a lot in common with some people from my wife's life, but John and Dawn were always friendly and fun. I didn't realize what great people they were until my divorce. I always jokingly say that I got custody of them in the divorce. They supported me and that meant the world. We had many good times after that, including camping each year at Jellystone Park and watching many Ohio State football games. Thank you both for helping me get through the tough days.

Judy

Judy was my brother's wife. She always took good care of my brother, and together they had a successful business, servicing MRI machines for hospitals, and a wonderful life. She stood by my brother's side throughout his illness, all the way until his death. She is godmother to my daughter, Julianna. She was my office manager for six years, and helped our dental practice grow from its infancy. My mother and I will always love Judy for being a great wife to my brother and I am grateful to her for still calling my mother "Mom", it makes her feel great. Thank you, Judy, for always being a part of our family.

Kim and Scott

Scott and Kim were the other couple who always supported me through one of the roughest times in my life. They are the type who always have something nice to say. They became patients and always bring a smile to my face when I see them. Some of our camping trips have become cult classics and they really do a great job inflating my ego when I am around them. It is always great getting together with them. Thanks, Kim and Scott.

Loretta

Loretta came into my life at just the right time. She was the personal trainer who taught me about good eating and working out. I loved our lunchtime workouts and talks. Loretta always listened and encouraged me, not only in health, but in life also. She has quite a life story that inspires me to this day. Loretta has helped in our "Complete U" seminars, doing the health and nutrition portion. She also got me on my Juice Plus product that I still use six years later. She and Brian, her amazing husband, fulfilled their lifetime dream and moved to North Carolina two years ago. Loretta will always have a special place in my heart for all she has done for me. Thank you, Loretta, I miss you.

Dr. Mark Braydich and Dr. Al Keith

I doubt there has ever been a trio of students like myself, Mark, and Big Al in dental school at one time. I am talking sheer size here. We all hovered around 6'3" and well over 220 (more now). We would have made a hell of an offensive line for the Browns. They were like big brothers to me in dental school, and the times I had with both of them will never be forgotten. They have played in my charity golf outing for the past sixteen years and, even though our golf games have gotten worse, our friendship will always be strong. There is something to be said for having people in your life who, just merely hearing their voice or seeing their face, takes you back to the good ole days and puts a smile on your face. Thanks, Mark and Al, for always being there for me.

Nichole

Next to my marriage, Nichole was the longest relationship I have been in. In three years, we did a lot of traveling, laughing, crying, dreaming, kid raising and business talking. Nichole is one of the most driven people I know, and she knows what she wants and works hard to get it. She has taken her dental placement service business to great heights and is very successful. She helped me through one of the roughest times in my life and I am grateful she brought stability, love and companionship to me when I needed it the most. I am glad that we still see and call each other from time to time. Thanks, Nichole, for always listening, understanding and being patient with me, I don't think I could have done it without you.

Dr. Stan Pechan

Stan is a dentist whom I casually met about fifteen years ago at CWRU. He was a one-day-a-week consultant. I found out he liked college basketball and asked him if he would like to go see some March Madness games with me here in Cleveland. He agreed, and 14 years and over 80 games later, we are still going to March Madness games all around the country. Throw in a trip to the Winter Olympics in Vancouver and the World Cup in Rio, and I guess you could call him my world traveling buddy. He also likes to kick my butt in tennis. Stan knows everything about everything. He is one of the most "worldly" guys I know. He has a newspaper in his hand no matter where we go, even if he doesn't know the language.

We have many more trips planned; Summer Olympics, Wimbledon, and who knows where else. Thanks, Stan, for taking care of me away from home. I love you buddy!

Dr. Steve Fox

Steve taught beside me in the clinics of CWRU School of Dental Medicine. We had a lot of fun in my nine years there. We became close friends and spent a lot of great times together. Steve is a computer wizard and helped me a great deal when I began my speaking gigs. He is now a full-time professor at the dental school, teaching young minds for the future. I miss my walks and talks during lunch with him and the other guys at the school. On occasion, I sneak up on him and do our jab in the ribs to remind him I am still around. Thanks, Foxy.

Sue

Not many of us can say they have an opposite sex friendship that has lasted as long as the one I have with Sue. We met in second grade and have remained friends for close to 40 years. We remained friends during high school, college, marriages, and children. She is godmother to my son, Matt. I know the When Harry Met Sally rule is that men and women can't be friends, but Sue and I are proof that it can happen. We never even dated. Sue helped me a lot when my marriage was breaking apart, by being a shoulder to cry on. I can never verbalize how much it has meant to me to have her in my life for so long. Thank you, Suey, Love you!

Susy

Yes, another Canadian. Many of the Croatians immigrated to Ontario many years ago, and my parents stayed in touch with them. My favorite was the Princ family. I spent nearly twenty summers traveling up "North" fishing and camping in Honey Harbour, Ontario. I also spent the better part of my childhood at Canadian/Croatian weddings. I really can't identify my dad's best friend but Susy's dad was pretty close to it.

Many times we grow up with people and don't realize how much we care for them until later in life, Susy was example of just that. I separate my "relationship life" to pre-marriage and post-divorce. Susy deep down in my heart was the first girl I ever loved. There were crushes and infatuations but nothing that felt as real as she did. She was the one that got away in the pre-marriage years. Maybe it was timing or maybe distance but it didn't work out. She has a wonderful life (recurring theme for the past women in my life LOL), with a wonderful family. We all keep many pictures of our childhood in our hearts and minds, and many of mine contain Susy. Thank you, Susy, for all the summers and always catching the biggest fish!

Dr. Tania Markarian

Tania is a great friend who in addition to being one of the most beautiful women I have ever met has taught me a lot about things like dressing correctly, designer clothes, manners (still has not sunk in) and, most of all, how to be genuine and passionate about everything in life. She is simply one of the kindest people I know.

Tania thinks and acts with her heart, a quality many people are moving away from today. We have similar lives, being single parents of three, and a lot of our talks revolve around the challenges of raising kids today. I don't think anyone can challenge me mentally like Tania can. She really makes me think and has taught me that opening your heart fully is still a good thing in this life. She has lived through many difficult challenges and in the end has always come out smiling. I really hope she writes a book about her life someday; it will be a best seller. Thank you, Tania. You are one of my dearest friends.

Tom

Every man needs a friend like Tom. Not only is he the smartest guy I know, he is also the most "worldly." Computer questions? Check. Music, trivia, money? Check, check, and check! What I am most grateful for is what an amazing husband he is to one of my dearest friends. He and Sue are godparents to my son, Matt, and have been there whenever I needed them. I think I burned Tom's ear off every day as my marriage slipped away. He always listened and told me I would be okay. Words mean a lot, but actions mean more. Tom has given me both in my life. Thank you, Tom.

Institutions

We can also be grateful for an institution or organization that has greatly affected us. The institution I wish to recognize is Case Western Reserve University in my home town of Cleveland, Ohio.

When I applied for admission to the pre-professionals dental program at CWRU in 1985, one of my father's friends laughed and said that I would never get in because that school is for the rich, snobby and only the smartest people in the world (he was bitter that his daughter did not get in the previous year). When I received my acceptance, my dad took the letter and disappeared. It was only later that I learned he had taken that letter and in a fit of pride presented it to the skeptical friend. I think it was the proudest day of my dad's life.

From 1986, the start of my undergrad, until my graduation from dental school in 1992, I walked the campus of this esteemed school. Soon after I returned and became a professor there, I have served on alumni committees and have met giants in many fields.

I will always love and cherish what CWRU has done for me. It has become my second home and to it I owe my allegiance and loyalty. I have donated money to it since my first year out, a mere fifty dollars back then. (It has grown since.....). Thank you, CWRU, for giving me the chance to prove myself all those years ago and still taking care of me today.

Special Tribute

This section is a special tribute to those key people in my life right now and probably will be for the rest of my life. One helped me through the dog days of college. Another is one of my two true lifelong friends, and the others are a daily part of my life now. I could not imagine my life without them.

Ken

This man has been my friend since the second grade at Roadoan Elementary School in Brooklyn, Ohio. We were known as "the kids that would not stop talking" in second and third grade, so much so that we were separated in fourth grade. My mother would return from parent/teacher conferences, and while I still don't know how much she understood of what the teacher said, one thing I know she got was, "Mario is a very good student, but he talks too much to Kenny." Kenny got the same report. We were reunited in fifth grade and that was a colossal mistake.

Popping the finger at a guy in a pickup on the way back from a field trip, the German slur, and whistling and yelling at a Raquel Welch commercial during library time were just some of the mischief we got into. We were also smart and artistic together, winning some art contests (he is by far the better artist) and putting together a massive D-Day display that stunned people. We were experts at imitating teachers and remembering every funny thing they said. We still remember those forty years later.

We went our separate ways for a while as far as school went, but always kept close. He was in my wedding and we play fantasy football together each year. When I was at my lowest during my divorce, he would come over and just try to make me laugh. Lots of times, he stayed over to keep me company (not in the same bed!). It's the moments like that when you know you can rely on your best friends. Every time I need to laugh or feel like the world was when we were just kids, I call Kenny. Thanks, Ken, for always being there. You are my lifelong best friend.

Dr. Tom Wilson

After the high school years passed, I got to the scariest part of my life, college and dental school. I thought I was pretty darned smart until I got to Case Western Reserve University. Being accepted into dental school out of high school on the condition that I would get nothing less than a B and complete all my prerequisites in two years of undergrad was no small task. Luckily, I found a friend in the first week of school who would become like a brother to me. I felt like I had found another Kenny.

Tom and I studied, laughed, cried and partied together for the next six years. He would become a part of my family, coming over many times to sleep and study since I was a commuter. He learned Croatian, and together we went everywhere and anywhere together. We went up and down his eight-floor dorm and were the school comedians and relationship consolers of many. The first question people always asked when they saw we weren't together was, "Where is Tom?" We were a regular Martin and Lewis, Abbott and Costello, Carson and McMahon.

The stories and times we had in those six years could and may fill another book someday. Tom and I should talk more than we do, but life gets in the way many times. Marriage, children and busy practices make for slim available time. I will never forget those years together, and if I knew he would be there, I would do it all over again. Thanks, Wilson!

Dr. Tom Thomas

If you listen to the dental gurus, they all say how difficult it is for dentists to be business partners. They say it doesn't work out for very long and usually ends up ugly. Well, it's been 20 years and counting for Tom and me. How is that, dental guru? I am not talking about "sharing space" partners, or "see you walking out and me walking in" partners. Tom and I have been 50/50 partners for 14 years, and we worked together for six years before that. We work together almost every day and sit in our shared private office a few feet away from each other. If we haven't killed each other by now, I think we will make it to the end.

We met in dental school and have known one another 25+ years. Again, the details and secrets of our success are for another book. Tom and I are different in so many ways, but very similar in all the important things, like love of family, love of taking care of people, and the love of laughing and enjoying life a lot.

Looking back at my dental life, I can't picture that I would have made it this long without him sitting in the same office with me day in and day out. I have often said that one of the greatest reasons I feel it has worked so well is that we have never tried to change each other, we accept who the other is and never let any petty things get between us. Oh yeah and a great belly laugh daily helps.

We took an RV trip from Cleveland to Yellowstone National Park a couple of years ago and it was one of my life's favorite times, just the dads and our kids on the road. It was only one of the great times we have had together in our lives and I know we have a lot more to come. Thank you, Tom, for being a great partner and a great friend for so long.

Dr. Ed Bice

There are always people in your life whom you wish you had met years sooner so that your time with them could have been longer. There are also people that you meet that you know you were meant to meet for a reason. As I stated earlier, Anthony Robbins brought me to some of the best people I know, and Ed Bice is the best of them.

We met in San Diego. The three-hour time difference made me get up at 5:00 a.m., and the place was so beautiful I decided to walk the grounds and "smell the roses" before the seminar started. Unbeknownst to me, Ed's luggage had been lost and he had no clothes to change into prior to the meeting. He was poised to get into the hotel store as soon as it opened at 6am to get some clothes. We both wandered out to check out the large patio where the day's breakfast would be served. We were the only two around and started talking. Four years later, we have not stopped talking.

Our families have spent spring break together in Florida every year since, and Memorial Day at their home on Lake Norman. They come visit us every year, and we golf and attend sporting events together. We talk at least once a week. Ed has become the brother I lost.

Our dreams and goals are similar, as are our love for family, learning and coaching our kids in sports (I in basketball, he in soccer). My family loves his beautiful wife Nicole and their incredible kids, Sierra, Bodie and Paris. Sierra just last year chose Julianna to be her confirmation sponsor. There is so much that Ed and I want to do to inspire and make this world a better place and we have started on that journey. I just hope life gives us enough time to accomplish all of them. Ed is one of the few people that challenges me mentally and makes me better than I could imagine and I will always be grateful that I woke up early that day in San Diego. Thanks, Ed, I look forward to the future together.

Dr. Ron Arndt

No matter how tough my dad was, I always loved him and wanted to make him proud of me. The life talks we had were pretty blunt and right to his point; there was not much I could say to him that could have swayed his opinion. He died ten years ago and, when a man loses his father, it leaves an empty hole that many times never gets filled. Dr. Ron Arndt has filled that empty hole.

Coach Ron, as he is known, was referred by a colleague and agreed to lecture in one of my classes several years ago. Since that day we have shared some of the best talks of my life, some of the best trips of my life and laughed harder then I could ever imagine. Our dinners out are epic, and the staff usually hands us the keys and tells us to lock up.

Ron has helped me learn so much and begin my journey in the coaching world. He and his wife Trish treat me like a son and I affectionately call him Dad. We have given incredible presentations together in front of many important people and brought the house down. Mutt and Jeff, Coach Ron calls us, and it is truly a horse and pony show. He listens to what I have to say (the coach in him) and doesn't judge, nor do I fear being judged by him. The stories of our lectures, trips and times could, and may, fill a book of their own someday (boy, I have a lot of books to write).

When something great happens, next to telling my mom and kids, he is the first one I call. I am so glad that he is in my life! Thanks, Coach Ron, for all you have done for me! Love You!

You have your List. Now what?

As you can see, I have many people on my list. Some from long ago, some from today. I have poured my heart on the page. And that gratitude helps me every day.

You can take several days, weeks even, thinking about who should be on your list and why. You can soul search, flip through old photo albums, and reminisce. The very act of thinking about gratitude can make you feel better.

Now is the time to use the guidelines in this book and have a list on a piece of paper. What should you do next? Nothing is worse than creating something and then never using it. After you have compiled as many names as you see fit to put on your list, it is time to integrate this gratitude into your daily life.

We have many things to be grateful for, our life, health, occupation and our situation in life. This list of people can be added to all that you have to be grateful for. This Gratitude List can be a list that gives you back more than you give it, maybe not in terms of something tangible or monetary, but in emotional gifts beyond your wildest imagination.

After you create your list, take some time and write out why they made your list. This exercise can open up all kinds of feelings.

You can also send them a note, explaining that you did a Gratitude List and why you choose to put them on your list. They will be moved and honored.

Then place the names into an Excel spreadsheet. You can separate them into categories, or simply list them alphabetically. In each person's row, enter their name, birthday, and any special days that you two have together (anniversaries, first day you met etc).

Next, you can place a spouse's name and their anniversary, their children's names and birth dates. It is really up to you how far you want to take it. For my closest people, I keep their birthdays, their spouse's name and birthdays and their kid's name and birthdays. This helps me remember to acknowledge them on their special day.

Depending on the size of your list, the names and dates can add up quickly. There will be people on your list to whom you are very close, and others that you have not talked to in years. You can decide how in-depth you get with each person.

After you have compiled the names and special dates, you must place them somewhere that will lead to action. You may be adept with phones, tablets and technology. Placing these important dates in your device will stimulate you to do whatever you have in mind to recognize them.

However, you may want to have a reminder a week before the actual event so you have time to prepare and mail, or plan a dinner, or whatever is fitting. For those of us who still like paper calendars, you can do the same kind of reminder system. I have a dedicated calendar only for my Gratitude List, where I have dates and what I did to celebrate them (so I don't necessarily copy it next year). I look at it weekly to remind myself of what is coming up.

This may sound like a laborious task that adds yet another thing to your daily chores, but you will probably find this fun and will be excited to contact and thank the people on your Gratitude List.

If it ever becomes something that is a pain to do and screws up your day, then please don't do it. However, I believe you will find that you will be delighted each day at the prospect of what the day brings. A birthday may be the only time that you talk to this person for the entire year. When you first start this, it may be the first time you have talked to this person in decades. Imagine the surprise they will experience too.

What if you sent a card with a picture of you two in college years ago with a caption saying that you have never forgotten them and what they meant to your life. These are actions that can impact a person's day, year or even life. This is the essence of the Gratitude List, spreading love and appreciation for the people who have meant the most.

Ideas

How can you express thanks and gratitude to these people? The sky is the limit.

You can also categorize your people into how you will thank them. Some will warrant an email or text on their special day you have identified. Next would be a phone call, then a birthday card, a special gift in the mail, a personal visit, a lunch, a dinner, a bigger gift. It will all depend on how close they live to you and how high they rank on your list. SendOutCards is a great way to easily send people a specific card.

You can scan an old picture of the two of you and send it off. You can purchase "thank you" cards in bulk to send to your list and say, "Thank you for being in my life and helping me become the person I am today."

Making people feel special is something that money can't buy.

You could gift them this book that has inspired you to create your list and include the story you have about them. Maybe it would spur them to create their own list and so on, one person to the next. My greatest dream would be that this book goes "viral" and everyone that has it in their hands creates a Gratitude List of their own.What an exciting world we would have if everyday every one of us would say thank you, in some way, to those who have meant the most.

Final Thoughts

A person seldom knows why his journey in life has taken him down a certain path. We many times understand even less where the path is going and to what end.

What I do know for certain is that every person in this book has been placed in my life for a reason. They have helped me become the man that I am and deserve every praise I have given them.

My hope is that by reading this book you not only create a Gratitude List for your life but also become a member of many others' lists. I hope you also realize how important you are in the lives of so many around you.

The small gesture, the seemingly insignificant words of praise and a simple "thank you" or "I love you" can reverberate in a person's memory for their entire life.

I am excited to see who will become the next member of my list and look forward to hearing from you about yours. I wish you every happiness that life has to offer. I wish you every adventure that the world can share with you. I wish for you to find gratitude for all you have been given and great memories of what has been taken away.

I leave you with one of my favorite quotes:

"Enjoy the little things in life, for someday you will realize they were the big things"

About the Author

Mario Pavicic, DDS, ACC

Dr. Mario Pavicic graduated from CWRU School of Dental Medicine where he is currently an assistant professor and director of the practice management courses. He is also a partner at Five Points Dentistry, a high tech, customer service oriented general dentistry practice in Strongsville, Ohio.

Dr. Pavicic, certified in customer service training from the acclaimed John Dijulius Secret Service Group, is also the only International Coaching Federation accredited dentist teaching at a dental school and is CEO of his own coaching business (www.pavicicdentalcoaching.com) where he coaches dentists how to run customer-focused based and highly profitable practices.

Dr. Pavicic is a graduate of the Anthony Robbins Mastery University and has assisted Tony Robbins during his presentations. Dr. Pavicic has developed his own highly inspirational personal development seminar called "The Complete U" which emphasizes Your Health, Your Wealth, Your Business and Your Life. For more information, visit www.the-complete-u.com.

Dr. Pavicic is a single father of three wonderful children, Julianna, Matthew and Nick, and lives in Ohio.

www.ingramcontent.com/pod-product-compliance
Lightning Source LLC
Chambersburg PA
CBHW060809110426
42739CB00032BA/3151